HOLIDAY COLLECTION

21st Century
Basic Skills
Library

WE CELEBRATE HANUKKAH IN WINTER

by Rebecca Felix

Cherry Lake Publishing • Ann Arbor, Michigan

1

Published in the United States of America
by Cherry Lake Publishing
Ann Arbor, Michigan
www.cherrylakepublishing.com

Consultant: Marla Conn, ReadAbility, Inc.
Editorial direction and book production: Red Line Editorial

Photo Credits: Kali Nine LLC/iStockphoto, cover, 1; Chris Kocek/
iStockphoto/Thinkstock, 4; Purestock/Thinkstock, 6; Noam Armonn/
Hemera/Thinkstock, 8; Jupiterimages/Photos.com/Thinkstock, 10;
Corvallis Gazette-Times, Andy Cripe/AP Images, 12; Kai Chiang/
iStockphoto/Thinkstock, 14; Charles Shapiro/iStockphoto/Thinkstock, 16;
yula/iStockphoto/Thinkstock, 18; Jupiterimages/liquidlibrary/Thinkstock,
20

Library of Congress Cataloging-in-Publication Data
Felix, Rebecca, 1984-
  We celebrate Hanukkah in winter / by Rebecca Felix.
    pages cm. -- (Let›s Look at Winter)
  Includes index.
  ISBN 978-1-63137-610-8 (hardcover) -- ISBN 978-1-63137-655-9 (pbk.) --
ISBN 978-1-63137-700-6 (pdf ebook) -- ISBN 978-1-63137-745-7 (hosted
ebook)
  1. Hanukkah--Juvenile literature. 2. Winter--Juvenile literature. I. Title.

BM695.H3F43 2014
296.4›35--dc23

                                    2014004491

Cherry Lake Publishing would like to acknowledge the work of The
Partnership for 21st Century Skills. Please visit www.p21.org for more
information.

Printed in the United States of America
Corporate Graphics Inc.
July 2014

TABLE OF CONTENTS

Eight Days

Hanukkah is a holiday. It is in winter. It lasts eight days.

Jewish people **celebrate** Hanukkah. They remember their history.

Light

Families light **menorahs**. They do this all eight nights.

What Do You See?

How many candles are lit?

Menorahs hold nine candles.
One is used to light the others.
A new candle is lit each night.

Songs and Games

People sing after the menorah is lit.

What Do You See?

People spin dreidels.

People play games with **dreidels**.

Gifts and Food

Family and friends gather.
Many give gifts.

What Do You See?

What food do you see?

18

People eat holiday foods.
Many are cooked in oil.

Hanukkah is a time to remember. It is a time of giving.

Find Out More

BOOK

Adler, David A. *The Story of Hanukkah*. New York: Holiday House, 2011.

WEB SITE

Hanukkah—Primary Games
www.primarygames.com/holidays/hanukkah/hanukkah.php
Learn more about Hanukkah through games and activities.

Glossary

celebrate (SEL-uh-brate) to enjoy an event or holiday with others

dreidels (DRAY-dulz) toys with four sides that are spun during a game of chance

menorah (muh-NOR-uh) a special candleholder used during Hanukkah

Home and School Connection

Use this list of words from the book to help your child become a better reader. Word games and writing activities can help beginning readers reinforce literacy skills.

after	foods	holiday	others
candles	friends	Jewish	people
celebrate	games	lasts	play
cooked	gather	light	remember
days	gifts	lit	sing
dreidels	give	many	songs
each	giving	menorahs	spin
eat	Hanukkah	nights	time
eight	history	nine	used
families	hold	oil	winter
family			

What Do You See?

What Do You See? is a feature paired with select photos in this book. It encourages young readers to interact with visual images in order to build the ability to integrate content in various media formats.

You can help your child further evaluate photos in this book with additional activities. Look at the images in the book without the What Do You See? feature. Ask your child to describe one detail in each image, such as a food, activity, or setting.

Index

About the Author

Rebecca Felix is an editor and writer from Minnesota. Many people there celebrate Hanukkah in winter. They have parties and special dinners. Some people go to holiday plays in the state's Twin Cities.